Immediate Action Marketting

Tactical Marketting System

Firearms Instructor's Guide
To creating a Magnetic
Marketting System

Omari Broussard

Copyright Page

Copyright © 2016 by Immediate Action Marketing

All rights reserved. No part of this publication may be reproduced, distributed, or transmitted in any form or by any means, including photocopying, recording, or other electronic or mechanical methods, without the prior written permission of the author, except in the case of brief quotations embodied in critical reviews and certain other noncommercial uses permitted by copyright law. For permission requests, write to the publisher, addressed "Attention: Permissions Coordinator," at the email address below.

ISBN-13: 978-1523802944 (978-1-5238-0294-4)

ISBN-10: 1523802944

Immediate Action Marketing
support@immediateactionmarketing.com
www.immediateactionmarketing.com

Dedication

This book is dedicated to my 3 younger Brothers: Will, Ojore and Tony. The dreams we can achieve are endless, if we just put our heart and soul into achieving them. I love you and I appreaciate the love you've shown me. Let's GET IT!!!

Acknowledgements

I'd first like to thank my Lord and Savior, Jesus Christ. Without His mercy and sacrifice I would not live the wonderful life I live today. To my wife, Tracee Broussard, thanks for being there with me through the good and bad times. For my children, this is just a small example of what it means to put yourself out there for the world to see. To my mentor and friend Rob Pincus, you've been the number one motivation in creating this book, hope you enjoy it. To the Combat Focus Shooting Instructor community, thanks for your support and asking great questions. This book was created for the CFS community first and foremost. To the Firearms Instructor community, I hope this book fills the gap and starts new conversations. To the "10X Mastermind", I got one! And last but definitely not least, Henry Evans and Lloyd Irvin! Thank you both for exposing me to the marketing world, I hope this book does you proud.

Table Of Contents

Dedication iii

Acknowledgements iv

Message from the Author vi

Introduction ....

Chapter One - 10 Principles of Immediate Action Marketing 1

Chapter Two - How to choose a target market and ideal client 11

Chapter Three - Becoming a "Weapon of Mass Attraction" 21

Chapter Four - The Rules of Engagement and Bonding with Your Audience 31

Chapter Five - Conversion: The Profitable Transaction of Value 43

Chapter Six - Delivery: Give your students an experience to rave about 60

Chapter Seven - Promotion Strategies 68

Conclusion 75

What's Next? 75

About the Author 78

BONUS Chapter #1: Basics of Building a High Converting Website 79

BONUS Chapter #2: How to leverage Strategic Relationships 94

Message from the Author

Dear Reader,

Hello!

First I would like to thank you for purchasing this book. I wanted to take some time to explain to you why I believe this book will help you.

I wrote this book because over the last 10 years I've been teaching personal defense I could not find any resource specifically written for firearms instructors on how to market and promote their business. This book is a culmination of 5 years of research, experimentation, testing, failing, and succeeding. I didn't invent anything in this book.

For the most part, the information in this book you can find going back as far as the early 1900's. However, it took me tens of thousands of dollars, numerous hours, and a large number of campaigns to get this information. Don't worry I enjoyed every dollar I invested and every hour I put in.

As I started to get a handle on marketing, many of my friends and peers started asking me questions. The most serious ones invested in my consulting services. One day I realized that no one else is going to focus on helping firearms instructors market and promote their business. So I raised my hand and took on the challenge.

This book is my first attempt at changing the way firearms instructors market and promote their training business.

This book is designed to be more of a conversation than a standard "How to" book. If we were sitting down in my hometown of San Diego, in my office, what you will read in this book would be our conversation.

This is book is the foundation.

I want to warn you upfront, marketing is work. It's something that has to be done every day. Every day you must get leads, sort through the leads to identify the buyers, give the buyers an experience, and persuade the buyers to bring you more leads. It's an endless cycle. But, you If you can systematize the process, you gain leverage. At some point, you will need to build a team (or outsource) in order to execute this system. That's okay!

So what if you just want to run a part-time training business? You can use these same strategies and tactics. Everything in this book has been proven to work. The system as a whole can be implemented in any business.

With all that said...

I want to congratulate you for taking this important step in your business. My goal is to help you take your business as far as you want it to go. If you are willing to put in the work, I am sure you will see results.

Have questions? Feel free to drop me a line at support@immediateactionmarketing.com

And remember to...

TAKE IMMEDIATE ACTION!

Omari Broussard
Founder, Immediate Action Marketing

INTRODUCTION

Have you Ever Wanted to have a flood of students throughout the year in your training courses? What about running a profitable firearms training business that provided for you and your family for years to come?

My name is Omari Broussard, and I can relate. Before I learned and implemented what I'm about to tell you in this guide I had:

- No marketing experience
- Limited business experience
- Wasted thousands of dollars on so-called "branding"
- And most of all no students to teach

Not to mention I had a full-time job (U.S. Navy), a father/husband, and I was going to college full time (working on a bachelor's and straight into a Graduate program). In addition to my lack of marketing knowledge, little money to invest in my new venture, I was determined to break new barriers as a firearms instructor...

I overcame this problem when I attended my first marketing event from a recommendation from a friend of mine. The event changed the way I thought about business, marketing and sales. But, it wasn't what I learned from the event that made the difference.

It was what I did after the event which made the major shift in my mindset and actions.

Once I got a handle on what you are about to learn in this book, I was able to literally chart my own course and I've even gone further to become a serial entrepreneur and consultant.

Here are just a few milestones I've hit:

- Feature on Fox News (twice)

- Interviewed on major podcast

- Interview on ESPN radio

- Published on Personal Defense Network

- Consulted companies in 6 different industries

- Trained high-level military, law enforcement, and security professionals across the country

- My own DVD sold by the top personal defense resource in the industry

- Retired from the military as a full-time entrepreneur

- And more!

i

I don't mention these milestones to brag, but to show you how this system and the thought process that underlies it will help you achieve whatever goals you are reaching for in your training business.

In this book, I'm going to show you how I did it and how you can too.

I'm going to do that by showing you how to choose a target audience, how to attract quality prospects, how to engage and bond with your prospects, how to convert prospects into high value students, how to deliver you training in a way that creates an experience for you students, and finally how to turn your students into Raving Fans that will promote you all over the country. [Note: You will also get a couple of bonus chapters]

By the time you finish this book, you'll have everything you need to build a foundational understanding of how a marketing system is built to deliver value and increase your profits.

Let's Get Started with **"The 10 Principles of Immediate Action Marketing."**

CHAPTER ONE

10 Principles of Immediate Action Marketing

If read nothing else in this book, this one chapter will serve you for years to come. One or all of these 10 principles are found in pretty much every marketing book, course you can find since the beginning of commerce. They are called principles because regardless of the industry, economic state, or company, you will find these to be constant in creating successful marketing campaigns.

- ✓ Principle #1: Marketing = Numbers x Psychology
- ✓ Principle #2: Marketing Formulas
- ✓ Principle #3: Market Awareness
- ✓ Principle #4: Market Sophistication

- ✓ Principle #5: Investment vs. Cost
- ✓ Principle #6: The Exchange of Value
- ✓ Principle #7: Only RESULTS count
- ✓ Principle #8: Business Stability and Profitability
- ✓ Principle #9: The 80/20 Rule
- ✓ Principle #10: Test, Test, Test

Principle #1: Marketing = Numbers x Psychology

I learned this principle from marketing legend, Dan Kennedy. The bottom line is that marketing is in fact scientific, it is Measurable, Observable and Repeatable. In order for you to master the science of marketing you must understand two things:

- The Numbers that come from measuring and tracking
- The Psychology of your ideal client

As far as the numbers go, your goal at the front end of your sales funnels should be to break even. Invest $1 in marketing to make a $1 back in profit. Once you can achieve the first goal, your next goal is to spend $1 and make back $2, and so on. This formula helps you to focus on judging your marketing success on the numbers and not get sucked into the latest and greatest "shiny object."

By understanding the psychology of your ideal client, you ensure you message will resonate with the prospects you want to attract to your business. Don't get sucked into believing your training is for everybody. Although you believe your training is for everybody, only a percentage will be willing to pay you for it. Focus on the buyers!

In crafting your marketing message, you must study the following:

- The market's awareness of your offer
- The market's sophistication
- The emotions that affects your market
- Your target markets buying behaviors

You can boil down the psychology of marketing by thinking about how humans develop healthy relationships with a prospective significant other. You have to meet before you date, you date before you get engaged, and you get engaged before you marry. It's the same process for turning a prospect into a client. Many business owners make the mistake of trying to get people to buy immediately. This is like asking a person to marry you on the first date. The successful businesses set up a system to facilitate the forming of a healthy relationship.

Principle #2: Marketing Formulas

In the previous principle, I mentioned that marketing is scientific, which means there are formulas you can leverage. The following are formula is found at the heart of every marketing strategy:

- Traffic + Conversion = Profit

Traffic + Conversion = Profit

I learned this formula from marketer and entrepreneur Lloyd Irvin. Traffic is the amount of eyes you get on your business. Conversion is the making the sale by converting prospects into buyers. The more traffic you get, the more opportunities you have to convert. However, the trick is to get the right traffic. All traffic isn't good traffic. By having a marketing system, you can compress the time it takes to attract quality traffic and convert prospects into buyers.

Converting prospects into buyers is the main focus of a systematic and results based marketing system. However, not all buyers are created equal. The key here is you want to convert qualified prospects into your ideal clients.

Principle #4: Market Awareness

Every business is subject to the market awareness model. The market awareness model was developed by Eugene Schwartz (author of Breakthrough Advertising).

Here is the breakdown (lowest to highest):

- Unaware
- Problem-Aware
- Solution-Aware
- Product-Aware
- Most Aware

Level 1: Unaware

The prospect who is unaware is the hardest to get. An unaware prospect has no idea they have the problem you can solve. Which means they have no awareness of your solution or your product.

Level 2: Problem Aware

The prospect is aware of the problem your offers solve, but may have little to no awareness of you or your business.

Level 3: Solution Aware

The prospect has awareness of their problem, and there is a solution to their problem. They may not know you have the solution, but they are familiar with the many options to solve their problem.

Level 4: Product Aware

The prospect is aware of the various products and services that will solve their problem.

Level 5: Most Aware

Prospects who are most aware may have already begun the process to solving their problem.

You want to focus your marketing efforts on levels 3 - 5. This portion of the market is significantly smaller than levels 1 & 2 but have the biggest chance of success. Remember, although your training may be for everyone, you will gain the most traction with the portion of the market who is actively aware and searching for your solution.

Principle #4: Market Sophistication

This principle is a continuation of principle #5. Every market has a level of sophistication. When you are developing your marketing message, you need to understand your market's level of sophistication. Here are the 5 levels of market sophistication:

- Level One: Your product is completely new.

- Level Two: Product is relatively new with some competition.

- Level Three: Market is inundated with ads but still has some unmet needs.

- Level Four: Competition is fierce. Competitors try to trump each other by being faster, cheaper, more convenient.

- Level Five: Market is Jaded. The market develop "ad blindness" and cease to pay real attention to advertising for the product or service.

Since this book is focused on the firearms instructor, you must look at the training industry a gauge the level of sophistication of your target market. For the most part, the market is sophisticated enough that all firearms training is not created equal. Based on the amount of advertising used to market firearms training, what are the unique aspects of your training that the market will resonate with.

Your marketing message needs to go beyond the features of firearms training (e.g. "I will teach you to shoot more accurately"). You need to dissect your training to find out what is the "Unique Mechanism" (a term I learned from marketer, Todd Brown), that will differentiate you or your training from your competitors.

Principle #5: Investment vs. Cost

Many instructors fall into the trap of believing that marketing is a cost. You need to look at marketing as one of the most important investments you can make in your business. Marketing is the one thing that gets you new business. Stop thinking about marketing as a cost and look at it as an investment. Which means when you think about marketing you will focus on ROI. Every piece of marketing material you produce needs to be judged by its ability to produce a return in the forms of new qualified leads and profit.

Principle #6: The Value Exchange

At its core business is about the exchange of value. This is true throughout the marketing and sales process. The ultimate value exchange occurs when a client is willing to give you their hard earned money. The more value you provide, the more your business will grow.

Principle #7: Only Results Count

There are a ton of tactics, strategies, models, tools and advice on how to market your business. It all comes down to what produces results and what doesn't. For this principle I will use a quote from Dan Kennedy from my favorite marketing book, "No B.S. Direct Marketing":

"The only votes that get counted are the customers' or clients', and the only bona fide ballots are their checks and credit cards. Everything else is hot air. From now on, you will be the most results-oriented businessperson on the planet, immune to criticism, or guesswork. If it sells, it's good. If it doesn't, it isn't."

Principle #8: Stability and Profit

Stability in your business is found in the amount of NEW business you are able to generate on the front end of your marketing funnels. Profitability is found in the back end of your business by getting your clients to purchase higher value offers or purchase more frequently. For the most part, you will spend most of your time developing various offers to get new clients. Once you get a new client, your job is to over-deliver and have offers in place to enhance their ability to achieve their desired result.

Principle #9: The 80/20 rule

The 80/20 rule is also known as "Pareto's Principle." It basically states that 20% of your efforts will deliver 80% of your results. Not only is this principle seen it business, but it is also seen in nature. Another point to bring up is 80/20 is fractal, which means it occurs until you run out of numbers. For example, if generate 1000 leads and 200 of them are converted into buyers. 20 out of the 200 buyers will spend more or spend more frequently. 2 out of the 20 will potentially pay for your highest priced offer.

Principle #10: Test, Test, Test

I had the chance to meet with Dan Kennedy at an event. I asked him with all his knowledge and experience in marketing (over 40 years and millions of dollars in revenue), how did he know if a particular marketing strategy or tactic would work. His response still resonates in my head today, "I don't know, I test, test, test." No one has a crystal ball, but what we all have is the ability to test. Going back to principle #9, it's been said by many high-level marketers, "80% of marketing campaigns you do will fail or fall short of its goals, it's the 20% of wins that makes you successful in business." How fast do you want to get to the 20%?

BONUS PRINCIPLE 0:

Before you do anything in this book, you damn well better be a good teacher, with a solid program. The community is small, I will come and find you! (I'm a Chief, I had to say it)

CHAPTER TWO

How to choose a target market and ideal client

In this chapter, we're talking about how to choose your target market and ideal client.

The things you need to focus on conducting research to find your target market and creating your "avatar". This is important to the entire process because before you start marketing your courses, you need to have chosen an audience that wants your services.

Most instructors are frustrated with the lack of people who are willing to pay for their courses. If that's not you then, you may have a percentage of prospects that take up your time, marketing dollars, and energy for very little return. By choosing a target market, you will ensure you are only putting your offers in front of people who are not only want you training but can also afford to pay for it.

The First Thing we you need to focus on is getting the research done. You will have to bear with me on this part, this is where my academic side may come out in the form of language. Okay, so here we go...

Market Research

When you are conducting market research, you will want to collect data on you perspective market. In the beginning, I will be talking about a group of people, but as we go on we will narrow it down to One person (remember this, it's important). There are three types of data you are going to want to collect:

1. Geographic
2. Demographic
3. Psychographic

Geographic data refers to the location of your market. It's important to narrow down where you are going to provide your training. In the beginning, you may start in your local area. I define "local" as within a 2-hour radius of where you teach. I want you to think about where your target market lives on a deeper level than just area. For example, I want you to look at area where the cost of living at a price point where the people can actually afford your training.

Also look at what type of areas are within your local radius, urban or rural. In your geographic study, I also want you to study your competition and complimentary businesses (ranges, gun retailer, outdoor store, etc.)

Demographic data will give you various data points on your market such as:

- Age
- Gender
- Marital Status
- Income Level
- Profession
- Family Makeup (children/no children)

Here is where we start developing a picture of the individuals you are targeting. Demographic data will help you to shape your ideal client or "avatar". I see too many instructors attempting to sell their courses to a person who doesn't' fit the makeup of the someone who is not interested in firearms training. More importantly this data will give you some insights on the type of people who have the ability to attend your training and pay according to the value you provide.

Psychographic data is the missing link for most instructors when deciding who they want to market too. **Psychographics deals with your market's behaviors.** Key things you want to look at are:

- What do they read?
- What do the watch?
- What internet sites they get information from?
- Who are they influenced by?

What activities are they current interested in?

Marketing is a combination of Math and Psychology. Don't make the mistake of not getting intel on what people are thinking and how they act. By understanding the psychographics you will have the ability to get inside the mind of your prospects and figure out what makes them decide whether or not to pay for your training courses (or products).

Once we finish with that, we will focus on Creating your "Avatar" (or Your Ideal Client). If you had to choose the type of student you wanted in your courses, who would they be? This one aspect of marketing was a Game Changer for me. Believe or not big consumer companies have a specific person they are targeting. Some companies have even given the person a name and a face.

Remember when I told you to remember the One Person? Here is where you create yours. I want you to think about your courses, what they provide and their price points.

Now I want you to take the data you collected from the previous section and create your ideal client. Think about who you would want to be your VIP...

- What is his or her name?
- Where do he/she live?
- How much does he/she make?
- Is he/she married? Children?
- What is his/her profession?
- What type of activities does he/she participate in?
- Have they taken a firearms course or is he/she brand new?

Does he/she own a firearm? If so, for what purpose?

You see where I'm going? Let's take it a step further?

- What keeps he/she awake at night? What do they fear?
- Who does he/she currently train with? Where does he/she train? Why

does he/she train there or with that instructor?

What publications, websites, etc. does he/she get information about firearms training from?

I know this seems like a lot but, before you move on, you must know this information. It's critical to your success.

Once you answer the questions, I want you to put it into story form...

Example:

Meet Jane. Jane is a 35-year-old single woman. She is a real estate agent in any town, USA. She lives in a condo and has lived on her own since she was young. She makes $70K/year and is looking to own her own brokerage one day.

Since becoming a Real Estate agent, Jane has had some close calls with violence. She is thinking about getting a handgun and concealed carry permit. Her decision was made due to reports of real estate agents being violently assaulted. She actually had one of he co-workers walk into a property where there were two people inside high on drugs and one of them made an advance on her.

She is currently looking into a basic handgun course, but would like to take a more comprehensive course on home defense and concealed carry. Since she is new to firearms, she has been reading material from the NRA and USCCA.

Blah...blah...blah (code for fill in the rest)

You get the picture. Once you are done, you will have one person to focus you marketing message on.

And finally, we get to focus on Research Tools...

You may have heard about the crazy thing called "Facebook". Most people use it to post videos of cute little kittens and air out their political views. I'm going to show you how to use it in a way that will help you make more money and get more students!

If you don't already have it, you need to setup a Facebook ad manager account. Head over to Audience Insights. In case you don't know, Facebook is a small business marketer's dream tool, but I digress.

Once you get into audience insights, type in a keyword into the "Interest box". You can use keywords like firearms training, handgun training, etc.

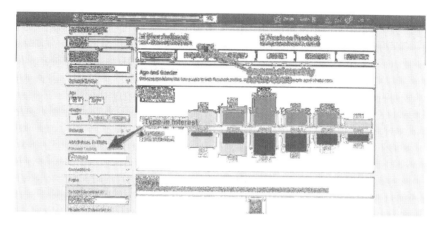

Take a look at your results and now you can start narrowing down your target market and ideal client. You can also see other things they are interested in. For example, in the photo above I now know that 30% of men on Facebook interested in Firearms Training is between the age of 35-44. 40% of women between the age of 35-44 are also interested in Firearms Training.

Here is a cool Marketer's Ninja trick...

You can click on the "pages liked" tab and look at pages your market is interested in. Click on a page, look through the post and comments and click on a person's profile. Now you can get a look at what your avatar would be like.

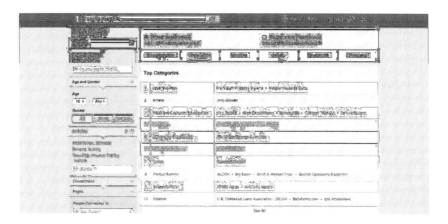

You can also use audience insights to look at your competition's market. Just type the name of your competitor in the "interest" box. You can get an inside look on the type of people your competitors are targeting. (This works if your competition has a large following).

Lastly, I want you to look at complimentary companies and influencers in the industry. The more information you have, the better. However, don't spend days trying to get everything. If you have already taught some students, you can pull them up on Facebook and create a target market and avatar based on your best clients.

Once you narrow down your target market and create your ideal client, you will set the stage for the messaging that goes throughout your marketing system.

In this chapter we Learned how to choose a target market and create an ideal client, by learning how to do the research, creating your "avatar" and using Facebook as a research tool. In the next chapter, we'll be covering **how to become a "Weapon of Mass Attraction"**.

CHAPTER THREE

Becoming a "Weapon of Mass Attraction"

In the last chapter, we covered how to choose your target market and the steps in doing solid research. Remember you want to start with who you are going to serve first and what you're going to provide second. Now that you know that we can start to focus on how to become a "Weapon of Mass Attraction" more simply put, how to attract qualified leads for your training business.

The things you need to focus on are being obsessed with providing value, incentivizing prospects to do business with you, and how to capture prospects information to continue the marketing process. This is important to the entire process because no matter how good your training is or how well you can teach if you don't have a system for attracting the right type of prospects, you will be DIW (That's Dead in the Water for your non-nautical types).

The first thing you need to focus on is making a conscious decision upfront to provide the maximum value possible for your prospects and clients. Many instructors think they are providing value, but I believe most don't until they get paid.

Here is what I mean...

In order for you to attract the right type of prospect, you will need to have the tools to give your target audience value upfront. Giving value, basically deals with giving your audience content that they can get a result from before they give you one penny. I've reviewed a ton of websites in the firearms training industry, and there is not many that use the important strategy.

I believe you can learn a lot from looking at what other businesses in other industries do to attract clients. Many companies spend thousands to millions of dollars in attracting first-time customers.

In fact, "Customer Acquisition" is one of the most expensive marketing cost in any business. If you were to break down the cost to get someone to give you the first sale you would notice the following:

- Cost to build a website

- Cost to attract traffic (pay per click, SEO services, Free traffic – which cost you time)

Cost of the first sale (especially if you discount your services on the first transaction)

I've also observed that most instructors don't maintain an email list which means they do not have a system setup to ensure they can keep in direct contact with prospects.

If you get anything out of the book, I want you to get this portion. Many small businesses suffer because they have either a lack of capital or a lack of new customers coming in. But, after you read this, you should solve the lack of new customers issue relatively quickly.

Before we get into the nuts and bolts of becoming a Weapon of Mass Attraction, I would like for you to think about the value you provide your clients. I could spend another chapter or so on value creation, but I'd like to defer to a marketing legend, Jay Abraham.

Jay Abraham is the author of the book, "Getting Everything You Can Out of All You Got." (I highly recommend you buy it). He is also the mentor of ultra-successful business owners. His core strategy is called the "Strategy of Preeminence" and the link below is to a video of Jay talking about this super important strategy.

You can watch the video here: https://youtu.be/SI6Rm07Hfls

You are probably asking yourself: "Why would Omari put a link to a video in his book." Because it's that important!

Did you watch the video? If not, promise me you will ASAP. If you did, congrats, you took Immediate Action!

Let's keep it moving...

When you focus on providing maximum value for your clients, you need to think about their "Ideal Transformation." When people come to you for instruction, they are expecting to have an experience that will take them from where they are to where they want to be. In essence, you are transforming them into their desired person.

Most instructors are setup to do a "one-and-done" classes. At the same time, they talk about how "perishable" shooting skills are, but they don't have a system in place that offers a client an A-Z solution. And I don't just mean live training, but also information products like books, DVDs, gear, etc. You want to be the "one-stop-shop" (or one-stop-resource) for all your clients.

That doesn't mean you have to be a jack of all trades. For example, let's say you provide concealed carry classes, but you don't have home defense classes. You could create a joint venture with another instructor (or get one on your staff) to provide the training you are deficient in.

The main point here is, do you provide just a "one-and-done" or do you provide a complete transformation?

Give your best upfront...

I've noticed that martial artist and firearms instructors are so afraid of giving away the "secrets." When you are obsessed with providing value, you will start with giving your best stuff upfront.

Incentives (Lead Magnets)

I want you to think about incentives as "magnets. More specifically "Lead Magnets", basically you need to create free offers in the form of pieces of content in exchange for an email address (or more contact information).

Why an email address? Because email is still a way of communicating with an individual on a personal basis. People still regard their email address as personal, like a phone number. I want to caution you to make sure when you are asking for email addresses you are in compliance with the CANN/SPAM list.

So what are some examples of Lead Magnets you can offer?

Here is a short list:

- Checklist
- Cheat Sheet
- PDF version of a blog post
- A number of responses from influencers on a specific subject (e.x. The Experts Say...)
- An interview
- A quick video tutorial
- A Free Report
- A live Webinar
- A video of you teaching a topic

A chapter of your upcoming book

An easy way to decide what to give away to your prospects is to listen to the most common questions you get. You are limited by your imagination and what your target market wants.

Use the lead magnets to begin a relationship with your audience. Remember you want to your audience to KNOW, LIKE & TRUST YOU.

Lead magnets are a great way to get your target audience to give you a "Micro-Commitment." Micro-commitments are a more efficient path to getting the sale. Here is how the process would work:

- You send an ad out on social media for your target audience to read a piece of your content. (micro-commitment #1)
- They read your blog post and within the blog post, you have an opt-in box for your Lead Magnet which requires an email address to access. They enter their email address. (micro-commitment #2)

Once you get their email address, you put them on a list that leads to an entry level course to get them started. (Commitment)

The point being, you know a person is committed when they may their first purchase.

As you can see, micro-commitments are a lot easier than just trying to get someone to buy your training cold.

One more thing...

Be sure to give your best stuff upfront! (Yes I'm repeating myself) You want your prospects to experience your expertise and the value you provide way before they give you money.

Capture Contact Information.

As I mentioned before you want to get the prospects email address, so you can continue the conversation. Now there are many ways to capture your prospects information:

1. Trading business cards
2. Someone calls your business
3. You get a referral
4. You hold a contest

You speak for an organization

However, the best way to collect an email is through an opt-in box.

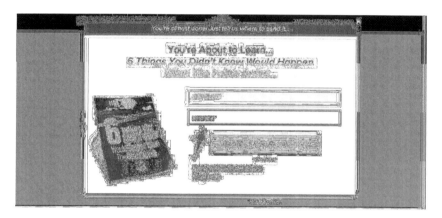

In order for you to legally send email to a prospect, they must give you explicit permission. An opt-in box can have text communicating to your prospect that they will be receiving relevant information. You can get a verbal, but to be on the safe side get your prospects to an opt-in box.

Opt-in boxes can be located on your website or on what is called a lead capture page (aka a "Squeeze Page"). Lead capture pages are basically a one-page website with one sole purpose, collecting email addresses. Lead capture pages are the most versatile webpages on the planet, and they work very well because it only gives a prospect one option.

Let's cover what the different levels of contact information you can collect. I use 3 levels of contact information:

1. Email address
2. Email address and mobile number
3. Email address, mobile, number, mailing address and credit card

The higher the level of information you collect the better. You can also gauge the level of commitment of a prospect by the amount of information you get. If you have level three information, you have a customer. I want you to get as much information as you can, but you have to be aware that the more information you ask for the higher level of commitment you are asking.

I want to highlight the mailing address. If you can get a mailing address, you have the opportunity to market to the prospect "offline" via direct mail. Direct mail can be expensive if you use it for getting leads. But, if you offer a mail delivered lead magnet (e.g. Free + shipping offer) then you can send postcard or letters to your prospects for follow-up. This is great way to maintain "Top of Mind Awareness."

Once you capture the contact information, you will want to maintain a database. This is achieved by using a Customer Relationship Management (CRM) system. At the lowest level, you could use a spreadsheet. There are a few email marketing services that also offer CRM software (i.e. Infusionsoft, ActiveCampaign, etc.)

In order to take your marketing system to the next level, you will definitely want a CRM. As of this writing, I use Infusionsoft as my primary and ActiveCampaign as a backup. Whatever you choose just make sure you actually use it to its full capabilities.

In this chapter, we Learned how to become a "Weapon of Mass Attraction" by learning to be obsessed with creating value, how you use incentives and how to capture contact information. In the next chapter, we'll be covering **The Rules of Engagement & Bonding with your audience.**

CHAPTER FOUR

The Rules of Engagement and Bonding with Your Audience

In the Last chapter We Covered How to become a "Weapon of Mass Attraction". Now that you know that we can start to focus on The Rules of Engagement & Bonding.

The things you need to focus on are The Rules of Engagement, The Introduction, The Bond, and Your Engagement Toolkit. This is important to the entire process because you will need to develop a certain level of trust with your audience before they commit to paying you for training.

The First Thing we you need to focus on is The Rules of Engagement. The rules of engagement focuses on one thing and one thing only...

Getting the person within your target market to trust you.

Trust is a very important aspect of business. If you want to build an army of raving fans who will purchase and support any program, product or service you create you first need to start on T-R-U-S-T.

A bulk of this section will be on the principles of developing trust by engaging and bonding with your audience. The last part will give you some suggestions on a few tools you can leverage to put the principles into action.

Here we go...

3 rules of engagement

I basically have 3 rules on engaging with an audience:

1. Be personable
2. Continue the conversation
3. Segmentation

Rule #1: Be Personable

I can pretty much write an entire book on this rule, but I'll keep it short so we can cruise through this because this is something you do every day.

When engaging and bonding with your prospects, you want to be yourself. People don't believe in companies they believe in people. The big take away is to be a person when you are selling your services. There is no need to use industry or corporate speak when telling people how you can help them.

I learned this rule from the famous copywriter, John Carlton, write you copy (emails, sales copy, Facebook ads, etc.) like you are having a conversation with a friend over a beer in a bar. Think about that for a second, if you were talking to a friend about firearms training you wouldn't use the normal industry speak. You would just tell them why you think training would help them and how.

Remember, the market doesn't care how good you are or how much better your training is over the other guy or gal. All they care about is how you are going to solve their problem. Keep this in mind when you are engaging and bonding with your market.

Rule #2: Continue the conversation

This may seem a bit weird but when you start a conversation you want to continue the conversation until there is a resolution. Let's say you meet someone at a network event and they ask you about a beginner's course for firearms. You take their email and put it on your list.

The email you send to your new lead should be about what they initially asked. This is an example of continuing the conversation. I find that when I sign up for an instructor's email list for free tips and updates, I get a schedule for their next course.

Good engagement is all about conversations with clear calls to action. A call to action is basically an offer, but an offer that is relevant to the initial conversation. We all know a good conversationalist, someone we can talk to and leads us to the next action. This is how you want to be in all your marketing.

Rule #3: Segmentation

Not all people on your list are created equal. Everyone on your list came to you for different reasons and for different offers. A big mistake in engagement is sending one blanket message to your entire list. A big NO NO!

You want to segment you list based on what interest they have. I'm taking a leap here, but I believe if you are reading this book you teach a number of courses (e.g. concealed carry, home defense, advanced skill development, etc.). Which means you have a number of segments to your business.

During the big ammunition crunch, I did a seminar to a Real Estate organization about the principles of self-defense. I couldn't just put those people on a list where my firearms training prospects were. I had to create a new list from which I could send relevant information to that list.

You can set up marketing campaigns to get people to raise their hands for different offers, but be sure you are segmenting your list. There is nothing worst then receiving marketing for stuff you didn't request.

The introduction

So what happens when you get a new email on your list? The first email needs to be an "Introduction" email. And your introduction email should be part of an Indoctrination Series.

I learned this tactic from Ryan Deiss at Digital Marketer. An Indoctrination Series is just a three email sequence where you introduce yourself, your company, your values and some of your best content.

This sequence of one of your core 3 email sequences you need to have in your email service provider. Below is a the breakdown of the Indoctrination email sequence (courtesy of digitalmarketer.com):

Email #1 (send immediately):

- Introduce yourself
- Whitelisting Instructions
- A reason to open the next email (a blog post or video)

Email #2 (send 1 day later):

- A picture of you doing something outside of shooting
- A link to the content you promised

A reason to open the next email (a Video or blog post)

Email #3 (send 2 days later):

- The content you promised from your last email
- A reminder to open future emails
- How to reach your team for questions

The indoctrination series is how you start the bonding process.

The Bonding Process

Bonding is all about getting your prospects to know, like and trust you. This is very important so don't overlook this process. If you want to transition from an expert to an authority, you will need to develop a relationship with your market.

There are a number of opportunities and platforms you will have the chance to bond with your audience. Here are the most important in my opinion:

- Teaching on the range
- Social Media
- Email

- Your Blog
- The Phone
- Direct Mail

Of course the range or in the classroom is where you are going to do your best bonding. The other five options are the main platforms where you can bond with you market before they pay you (which is what marketing is all about).

I believe email is the number one place to build the bonding process. It doesn't cost much (although you should treat it as though it is expensive), it's more controllable, and it's considered personal to your audience.

I can honestly say I've made more money with email than any other tool in my marketing arsenal. There are 7 figure businesses being built via email.

Through your emails, you develop a relationship with thousands of people around the globe. Here is the trick to bonding over email. You might want to circle the next sentence in green pen (green for dollars)...

WRITE 99% OF YOUR EMAILS IN A CONVERSATION TONE!!!!

Remember email is used for personal communication. You want to bond with your prospects on a deeper level so write them as if your were writing to a friend. I promise you your list and your business will LOVE you for it.

Before we move on, here are some ideas for what to send you email subscribers:

- Training tips
- Gear reviews
- Updates on course
- Client (student) success stories
- Lessons learned
- Articles on training
- Blog updates
- Offers
- Personal stories

And finally we get to focus on your Engagement Toolkit.

You engagement toolkit are the tools you will use to engage and bond with your list.

You are going to need three tools to engage with your list:

- Social Media Account
- A blog
- Email service provider

Social Media account

I don't think I need to explain what the different types of social media platforms exist. But I do feel compelled to tell you how to determine which one you should use.

When trying to determine which social media platform to use, determine which one your target market uses and responds to most. It's that simple. For the most part, you can't go wrong starting with Facebook. Facebook has 1.3 billion users, which means most likely your market is there. However, you have to be aware of the conversation happening on Facebook.

I find Facebook to have the best advertising platform of all the social media providers. Facebook is a great place to share your content and then use it's "re-targeting" feature to build list within the Facebook advertising platform to send ads to.

Although there are a significant number of the world's population on Facebook, most of the conversations are social not business. Statistics show that audiences on Pinterest are more geared towards buying vs. Facebook.

What if you are going for a more corporate or b2b audience? Then LinkedIn may be your social media platform of choice. LinkedIn is also known to have the audience with the highest net worth.

Bottom line is to go where the market is.

A Blog

Your blog should reside on your home website. It should also be the home of all your content. When you display your expertise and knowledge, do it on your blog. Your blog will also have your opt-in for your lead magnets and email list.

You can have all types of content on your blog:

- Video
- Articles
- Powerpoints
- Audio

Your blog will also help you to rank on google for search results. It pains me to see a firearms training company without a blog. Along with your email list, your blog is one of the most powerful tools you have at your disposal. Please, Please have a blog.

Use your social media platform to promote your blog content. You want to leverage your social media to get people to your blog. Then use your blog to get people on your email list.

Email Service Provider

Email service providers give you the power to communicate with your list behind the scenes. You can use your email provider to do the following:

- Follow-up
- Introduce offers
- Ascend your clients up the "value ladder"
- Long-term nurture
- Educate your list
- Give updates
- Give special discounts
- And more!

There is really no limit as to how you can use your email system to serve your audience.

Here are a couple of tips to maximize the value of your email marketing system:

- Ensure you follow the rules for email marketing. Email marketing is permission based, be sure you get explicit permission from your prospect to be on the list.
- When a new person is added to your list, ensure you have an "indoctrination sequence" setup, so

you build a bond with your new subscribers.
- Be sure to segment your list based on their wants and interest.
- Treat email as if you are paying per email sent. Just because sending email is low cost, treat it like it cost.
- Here is a list of popular email service providers:
- Aweber
- Mailchimp
- ActiveCampaign
- Infusionsoft

Email marketing system vary in cost due to the softwares capabilities. I am a fan of those who have a significant level of automation and segmentation. To watch a video on my favorite ESPs click the link below:

In this chapter, we Learned how to Engage and Bond with your audience by learning the "Rules of engagement", how to indoctrinate your new leads, how to develop trust with your audience, and your engagement toolkit. In the next chapter we'll talking about **how to convert your prospects into buyers (paying students)**.

CHAPTER FIVE

Conversion: The Profitable Transaction of Value

In the Last chapter, we covered The Rules of Engagement and Bonding. Now that you know that we can start to focus on how to How to convert prospects to clients.

In This chapter, we're talking about the sales process for getting prospects to pay your for your training courses, products, and services.

The things you need to focus on are Offers, the 5-step marketing and sales system, and the key elements of your sales message. This is important to the entire process because it's good to build an audience, but the goal is to build an audience that trusts you enough to pay you for your services. The only good list is a list that is monetized.

The First thing we you need to focus on is offers. In order for you to convert a prospect to a buyer is by creating and promoting offers. As discussed earlier in the book, one type of offer is your lead magnet. Once again, a lead magnet is an offer of value to a prospect in order for them to give you an email address.

There are three other offers I want you to be aware of:

1. A Self-Liquidating Offer
2. A Core Offer
3. A Higher Value offer

A self-liquidating offer is also known in the marketing world as a "tripwire." It's an offer that gets a buyer for a low cost. For example, if you were to offer a video series (or e-book) on how to choose a defensive handgun for home defense at $7. You've created an offer that could solve a problem for your list at a price point that doesn't' take much thought. It's pretty much an impulse buy.

I want you to get a clear understanding on the purpose of your self-liquidating offer. The money made from your self-liquidating offers are to help you cover the cost for the traffic (and to get you more traffic). This is an important marketing principle to remember:

"The one who can spend the most on traffic, WINS"

The trick to crafting effective SLOs is to take a "splinter" of your Core offer. You could take your 1 full day or 2-day course and offer a 4-6 hour version at a lower price point. Or you could take the lecture portion of your course and offer a webinar version.

Core Offer

Your core offer is the offer you have that will give your clients the most value and the ideal transformation. For example, in a firearms training business, you core offer maybe your 1 day or 2-day course because it gives you the optimal amount of time to help a person develop the skills necessary to handle and use a firearm.

A splinter of your core offer maybe a video series on how to choose a defensive handgun and recommended range gear for firearms training. The video series is a "splinter" of what they will learn in the full course. As you can see the SLO is a relatively quick way to get a desired result.

The High-Value offer

I believe every business owner should have a "High Value" offer. One reason is because it raises the perceived value of your business. Secondly, because there is a portion of your market who will pay premium prices for premium service.

In the firearms training business, most high value offers come in the form of advanced training courses or specialty course. Private courses are another way of offering higher value. You can also offer a VIP service to your clients.

A good example of a high-value offer is from Apple. When Apple created the Apple Watch, they created a top tier watch at the price point of over $10,000.00. Apple knew most people wouldn't purchase it, but they also knew there was a segment of its market that would want the status of having one of the most coveted watches in the world (at the time the Apple Watch was introduced). This may seem out of reach for most but think about it.

What if you offered a 3 Day VIP Course weekend, which included lodging, range gear bag and tools, dinner, and other cool gifts and your charge $7000.00 per person. Even if you only get 3 people to attend, you get a $21,000 gross weekend. Use your imagination to create the ultimate experience and charge accordingly.

Other offers you can use to maximize profit

In addition to your core offer, you can use upsells and down sells and to increase your clients value.

Upsells are offers you attach to a core offer. Let's say you offer a 1-day shooting course. When a client purchases the course, you offer them an additional product or service before they reach the checkout page from the first offer. Think of something that will help them get to their desired result faster or better. For example, the buy a concealed carry course, you can upsell them a skill development course or DVD.

Down sells involve offers that are lower cost than the upsell. For example, you offer the DVD, and they say no, then you offer them a lower priced item like a range cleaning kit.

You don't have a range cleaning kit? You can look into becoming an affiliate for a company that does. Affiliate programs are used to help companies develop a sales force. You can get commissions on selling products from other companies. These are products you can add to your sales funnels to help increase the value of your customers.

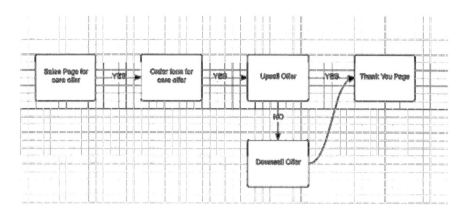

(Sales Funnel example with Upsell and Downsell)

Affiliate products can also be used for cross-selling. Cross-selling is where you offer a product or service in another domain. For instance, you offer the buyers of your concealed carry course a home defense DVD course. Even if you don't have a home defense course, you may find another company that has one you believe in.

[NOTE: In order to use the upsell/downsell option check with your shopping cart provider]

Now I'm going to show you how to craft a sales funnel that will house your offers and deliver them in a systematic way...

The 5 step marketing and sales funnel

Step 1: Identify Product Benefits

Step 2: Identify Target Audience

Step 3: Create the Offer

Step 4: Capture Information

Step 5: Convert

Identifying the Product Benefits

What are the benefits of your products? The benefits focus on what your courses or products can do for the client. Many times benefits are confused for features. A feature is what the product or service does. Benefits are what the product and service can do for the client.

Your prospective client has two states of mind: The before state and the after state. The before state is the state the client is before they purchase your product or service. The after state is the desired state they wish to be in.

Your benefits are geared towards the after state. You marketing messages should be focused on how you can give your client their desired after state.

Next, you want to list the problems your product or service solves. As business owners, we help clients either increase their status or solve a problem. By increasing their status I mean, we help the go from one state to another. For example, you may take a beginner to an expert. Beginner and expert are two different states in the firearms training world.

We also solve problems. Problems many people face when it comes to firearms instruction are helping them to choose the right firearm for them, how to employ a firearm for recreation, competition or personal defense. There may also be other problems they are trying to solve, which you have the knowledge to help them. For instance, if you teach a concealed carry course, that helps people qualify for a state mandated qualification. You also have the ability to help them develop the skills to be more aware of their surroundings, even if they are unarmed. With that knowledge, you could create an online course on "Situational Awareness in Public."

There are many opportunities to demonstrate your value and expertise when you focus on helping your prospect change from an undesirable state to a desirable state and solving your prospects problems.

Once portion of product benefit identification I find many instructors overlook are the emotional triggers, your product or service invokes in a prospect. The key emotional triggers are as follows:

- Fear
- Gain
- Logic
- Status

Fear is the ultimate emotional trigger, but should be used sparingly. I'm not a fan of preying on a prospects fear in order to sell a product or service. However, it does play a part in how people make buying decisions. Studies show that people are more inclined to go with the options that help them "avoid pain" vs "giving them pleasure."

Personal defense is driven by fear: fear of loss, fear of conflict, fear of being a victim. I believe the way to use fear in marketing firearms training is the education on how to understand and utilize the benefits of fear in a personal defense situation. We can not eliminate fear, but it can be managed in a healthy way.

Gain is an emotional trigger that makes people feel like they achieved something. People feel good when they are gaining knowledge and resources. In the firearms training arena you can explain how your training will help them gain a sense of security and confidence.

Logic is a way for you to explain how your offer makes sense to have. In the buying process, logic is how we rationalize our buying decisions. For instance, if a person has purchased a firearm it's logical to be trained as much as possible in it's use. Remember this, people buy on emotion and use logic to rationalize the buying decision. So in your marketing message lead with emotion and support them by using logic to justify the buying decision.

Status is also an emotional trigger. People are inherently social beings. In any society there is a sense of status. You may have heard the term, "Sheepdog". This term denotes a level of status in society. A sheep is a person that is oblivious to the danger around them and is susceptible to being prey to the wolf. A wolf is someone who preys upon the sheep with no moral or ethic code. A sheepdog is one who is willing to sacrifice their life against the wolf to protect the sheep. At it's core the sheepdog has the knowledge, ability and skills to protect the sheep from the wolf. This is more or less a "status" play. Being a protector versus a victim is also a status play.

Identify your target audience

There is a reason why the first chapter of this book takes a deep dive into determining who your target market is. As you craft your marketing and sales campaign you will want to ensure you have your target market and ideal client in mind.

As you dissect your training courses, you will notice each course you offer may have its own target market. There is also the option to have a target market in mind as your course offerings evolve and expand.

For example, you may decide to customize a course for a certain demographic. In my experience I noticed that some of my courses appealed to a certain type of market and I had to massage the messaging to the meet the needs of the target market.

Knowing how to reach your target market is important. As the great hockey play, Wayne Gretski would say, "Go to where the puck is." You want to go to where you market is.

Create Offers

Once you have the product benefits down and you have a target market, now it's time to start creating your offers. You will want to create your offers in the following order:

- OFFER #1: A lead magnet that offers a specific solution to a specific problem
- OFFER #2: A low barrier to entry offer that gets a buyer, fast (this is optional)
- OFFER #3: Your core offer
- OFFER #4: Offers that increase the frequency of purchase and/or increases the buyers value
- OFFER #5: A high ticket offer to increase your company's perceived value and is designed for the top 2% of your market (optional, but highly recommended)

Capture prospect information

You are going to use your lead magnets to capture prospect information. Refer back to "Becoming a 'Weapon of Mass Attraction'" for the 3 levels of contact information you are trying to capture. Remember, each level of information demonstrates the lead's level of commitment throughout the buying process.

Convert

Conversion is all about getting the sale, delivering an experience and implementing offers 4 and 5. I learned this important principal about sales from Dan Kennedy, "You don't make a sale to get a customer, You get a customer to make sales." What he means is once you get a sale you now have a customer to which you can present them with more opportunities to raise their status or solve a problem in the form of offers, thus getting more sales.

And finally we are going to focus on the 12 elements of a high converting sales message.

The key in writing a high converting sales message is to craft your words into a message that motivates your prospect to take a desired action. In this case the ultimate action is to get your prospects to spend money with your business (or get on your list).

We are going to accomplish this by "copywriting." Copywriting is basically "Salesmanship in print." Although there are many philosophies on how to write high converting copy I was able compile a few resources together to give you a model on how to create great copy.

Copywriting is a skill you should learn, develop and master, because it is responsible for creating the best results for any business.

Your sales message must be geared toward overcoming objections and persuading your prospects to take action. Regardless how long or short you sales message is, you will need to know and understand the following elements in order to be successful in generating sales messages that lead to action.

The 12 elements of a high converting sales message:

Get Attention

   a. You want to get the attention your prospect by creating an attention getting headline

Identify the problem

   a. You want to speak to the problems your target market is having.

b. Agitate the problem so they feel compelled to take action

c. Use a short story to explain the problem

   Provide the Solution

a. Explain how your solution is the answer to their problem

   Present your credentials

a. Notice we did not start off with how great your company is or your expertise

b. Now is the time to tell the prospect your qualifications

c. Use case studies of how you solved the problem for others

d. Show your authority in the market

Show the Benefits

a. Give bullet points on the benefits of your training

b. Remember: people don't care about you or your product. They care about what you and your product will do for them

Give Social Proof

a. Build your credibility and believability

b. Use success stories from current or past clients to demonstrate your solution and expertise

Make your offer

   a. Give them in "irresistible offer"

   b. Add bonuses or premiums

   Give a Guarantee

   a. Take the risk out of the buying process

   b. The stronger the guarantee the better

   c. If your offer seems to good to be true explain why

   d. Guarantees demonstrate the confidence you have in your offer

Inject Scarcity

   a. Use and extra incentive to motivate prospects to take action

   b. Give a bonus to those that sign up immediately

   c. Offer limited spots

   d. Give a deadline for the offer

   e. Offer a discount to those who take action immediately (limited to a number of people of course)

Call to action

a. Give step-by-step instruction on the order process

b. Don't take for granted they will know how to purchase

c. Sprinkle your call to action throughout the sales message

Give a Warning

a. Give your prospects the consequences for not taking action

b. Show them what they will miss out on by not taking this offer

c. Go back to the emotional triggers

Close with a reminder

a. Use a P.S. line to summarize the offer and reinforce the benefits

Some shortcuts to crafting a high converting sale message:

- Keep a file of successful sales messages inside and outside your industry (use for inspiration and modeling)

- Start by writing down the features and benefits of your courses and/or products

- Focus on writing your message to your ideal client. You want to attract your ideal clients and repel your unwanted prospects.

By following and practicing this model you will craft sales messages that grip your prospects and compel them to taking action.

As a side note, not everyone will buy your courses. But, having a good sales message will ensure you are helping your prospect make a solid decision on whether or not they want to purchase from you. I find that the number one way to one up your competition is to craft a compelling sales message that speaks to the emotions and logic of your ideal prospect.

In this chapter we Learned how to convert prospects to buyers by learning the different types of offers, The 5-Step marketing and sales blueprint, and the 12 key elements of a marketing message.

In the next chapter, we'll talking about the benefits of **delivering an experience for your students**.

CHAPTER SIX

Delivery: Give your students an experience to rave about

In the Last chapter, we covered types of offers, the 5 step blueprint for a marketing and sales campaign, and a model for writing high converting sales copy. Now we can start to focus on how to how to deliver your service with the poise and experience of a "Broadway Show".

In This chapter, we're talking about the principles of delivering a memorable experience for your clients.

The things you need to focus on is the principles of over-delivering, crafting a memorable experience, and crafting a client journey within your business. This is important to the entire process because your ultimate goal is to build an audience of "Raving Fans." The experience you create for your clients will go a long way to doing exactly that.

The first thing you need to focus on is the principle of "over-delivery". I'm assuming you already have a course that gives more value than what the client paid for it. But, I want to just take some time over the next couple of pages to give you some tips on how to leave a lasting impression on your students.

I want you to think about what are the things you can do to under-promise and over-deliver.

Here is a quick story to explain my point...

I ordered a red dot sight mount for my Aimpoint T1 (happens to be my favorite optic). I spent a significant amount for the mount but given who I ordered it from I knew I would get a quality piece of equipment.

When the mount was delivered, the company went above and beyond. I also received a copy of the U.S. Constitution (I had lost my other copy, so this was a welcomed addition), a cool bottle opener, and a bottle of the company's own bbq dry rub. If you've ordered from this company, I'm sure we had the same experience. In fact, when I'm hanging with other instructor's across the country we all talk about the bottle opener and the seasoning.

This is an example of under-promising and over-delivering. How can you give more value to your client when you deliver you products or training courses.

Here is a quote from the great Earle Nightingale, "When you are in a space of which you are unfamiliar look at what everyone else is doing and do the opposite." (paraphrase).

For the most part, every firearms instructor gives decent training in the eyes of most people. So if you are perceived as having comparable training how do you over-deliver? Here are some ideas:

- Give framed graduation certificates
- Give clients a custom challenge coin (challenge poker chips are also a cool gift)
- Have water and snacks available at no cost for your students
- Bring extra cleaning kits (give them away)
- Have lunch catered at the course (maybe include this as a VIP option)

- In addition to a course certificate, give an "Alumni" gift like a coffee mug or shot glass with your logo on it

- Create a special t-shirt for students

These are just a few tips for you to use. In case you are wondering you should not come out of pocket for the "extra" items. Pass along the cost of the extras into the cost of the course. You can get the extra "premiums" at a relatively low cost. Think about getting sponsors for your courses so they can help cover some of the cost to get their brand introduced to your clients (Caution: be sure you believe and support your sponsors brand and products)

Crafting an experience

Most people can relate to the experience of a Broadway show, but for those who can't, I'll give a brief explanation. A show that makes it to broadway must be entertaining and also invoke true feeling in the audience. Plays and performances that make it to a broadway stage are perceived as the cream of the crop. All the shows have actors, scripts, and a flow that takes the audience from certain state and leaves them in a desirable state, one that feels happy and entertained (unless it's a tragedy story.)

The point is you want to craft a flow to your courses. After teaching hundreds of courses and thousands of students, I've become quite particular about how my courses begin and end. Here is an example:

- I have my director of operations lead the setup of the range

- My executive assistant takes care of greeting the students and ensures the proper paperwork is completed.

- Once it's go time I make my entrance and greet everyone with a smile, learning everyone's name.

- Intro brief begins in the staging area.

- Everyone grabs their gear and we meet on the firing line to do the safety brief.

- Throughout the course there is mandated Q and A times

- When students go on break, I go on break

- Lunch is a time where break bread and get to learn more about each other.

- I introduce the more dynamic drills in the afternoon so the students leave on a high point

- We do a lengthy debrief at the end of the day, so the clients leave with their questions answered.

- I give every student an "Alumni" gift
- Ask for testimonials and get them on video or audio (remember social proof?)
- I make an offer for the next course (or related products)
- We take a class picture, which I make available to the class.
- We high five and hug, wishing each other safe travels

This is the framework for all my courses and 10 out of 10 times I get rave reviews, Facebook posts, and high praises, but it doesn't' end there.

Once we get back to the HQ my staff gets to work on the behind the scenes follow-up using our automated marketing systems.

I also review my performance for the day to see what we can tweak to make it a better experience for the clients.

By the end of the course I not only have happy clients, but more importantly I have new converts, who've become part of my "tribe." I still get gifts and praises from clients I've had in course years ago.

What does your "broadway" show look like?

Another example is Disneyland. Disneyland is the known as the happiest place on earth because of the way Disney has crafted the experience. Not just at the park, but it's movies, DVDs, cruises and time shares. Everything is scripted and performed at the highest level.

The Client Journey

Another way for you to ensure you are delivering the ultimate experience is to have a client journey in mind.

Your client journey is based on how you can take them from where they are to their ultimate self. I look at all my students (clients) who come to me for personal defense training and think about how I can make them the biggest bad-ass on the planet when it comes to dealing with violence (at all levels). I don't just look at the shooting, I also look at how I can improve their verbal skills, decision making, first aid, natural disaster survival, communications, vehicle safety, etc. I look at all facets that make up a true warrior.

I deliver both on the range and off the range. They learn skills from me in my blog post, videos, content from other authorities in the industry. I give them access to information from my mentors and teachers. I hold nothing back. No Secrets.

Don't misunderstand me, this doesn't mean I give away the farm for free. I release access to information in the form of content which leads to offers. How do you take a new person to your training and give them the ultimate experience?

In this chapter, we Learned how to deliver the ultimate experience by learning about the importance of "over-delivery", how to craft an experience, and developing a client journey. In the next chapter be talking about different **promotion strategies for your business**.

CHAPTER SEVEN

Promotion Strategies

In the Last chapter we covered the importance of Over-delivery, Creating the Ultimate Experience for your clients, and the client journey. Now that you know that we can start to focus on some key promotion strategies.

In This chapter, We're Talking About 3 ways to promote your training company. Although this entire book is about promotion, but I wanted to break out 3 ways to promote your business after delivering a great experience.

The things you need to focus on are asking for referrals, getting social proof and leveraging the media. This is important to the entire process because many instructors fail to maximize the opportunities to get more business by leveraging their happy clients. Believe it or not, the best way to acquire new clients is to leverage existing clients to do the work for you.

Asking for Referrals

Referrals are the best way to maximize the value of one client. Getting your happy clients to refer you and your business can result in getting multiple clients for the price of one. Remember the most expensive cost in your business will be acquire new clients.

So how do you get more referrals? You just Ask! Many instructors fail to ask clients for referrals. If you have been to a gym like 24 Hour Fitness, you have been exposed to a business that asks for referrals. In fact, I'd wager to say, 24 hour fitness has a specific system for generating referrals for everyone who becomes a member or visits a gym for the first time.

Let's look at how we can "swipe & deploy" their system...

I can remember when I was younger I was invited by a friend to visit their gym. When I arrived, I was given a tour and allowed to work out. Before I left the clerk at the front desk offered me some free passes for my friends. The free passes gave my friends free access to the gym for a day.

Now that I think about it, it was genius of them to give me the passes.

Now how can you model their referral system? You could give your clients 3 passes for their friends to attend your next entry level course at a discount. You know I'm not a fan of discounts but, check this out.

Let's say your entry course is $150. To get a new client to pay you $150 it may cost you anywhere from $50-$100 in marketing costs (time and money). By giving your client 3 passes for your entry course at $97 you can get 3 new clients for zero marketing cost without having to spend a dime in marketing. You lose $53 in gross profit, but you gain a client at $97. To take it a step further, you gain 3 new clients at a profit of approximately $300. You invested $50-$100 in getting the first client. In return (pending everything works out), you get 4 clients and a total of $441 in gross profit (roughly).

This is just one strategy to getting referrals for your business. You can put together 2-3 strategies for generating referrals and exponentially increase your revenue.

Take some time to jot down ideas for generating referrals in your business. If you have trouble coming up with referral generation ideas, just take a look at other businesses to see how they do it and model their strategy. Sam Walton, the founder of Walmart, was known for visiting other stores to get an inside look at how the retained and acquired customers. We can learn a lot from a guy like Sam Walton.

Social Proof

The saying goes, "People don't believe much of what you say, but believe more of what others say about you. Both good and bad."

In the new economy business is more personal. The internet allows consumers to give real-time feedback on their experience with any business. This can be bad or good. Bad because people are more prone to publicize a bad experience. Good because people are prone to publicizing an outstanding service experience.

Platforms like Google Places and Yelp give consumers the opportunity to publicized their thoughts on how well they were treated by any business. The bottom line is you want to leverage the power of social proof.

Testimonials, success stories, and case studies are a great way for you to highlight your clients and their experiences with your business. You want to have social proof throughout your digital and offline marketing platform and material.

Think about the movie industry. How many movies have you watched just based on the word of a good friend? Movies make millions of dollars just off social proof. And you can too!

You want to program in a time for you to get testimonials and success stories during your courses. People love to give their opinion, just ask if your clients wouldn't mind giving their opinion on their experience with your material.

Video is the best way to collect testimonials. Once you get the video, strip out the audio and have it transcribed into text. Use the video and text testimonials everywhere you can. The more the better!

And finally we get to focus on **leveraging the media**.

There are many opportunities for you to leverage the media and get more exposure. Local media is always looking for experts on various topics to help them give the community relevant and valuable content.

Featured on Fox News in New York City. Courtesy of Fox News)

Getting your company in the media can go a long way in building your authority in the industry. Here are some example media outlets you can leverage for your business:

- • Local and National TV
- • Online and Offline news publications
- • Industry Blogs
- • Podcast
- • Community Newspapers
- • Industry newsletters

You can write articles and have them syndicated. Press releases are also a way you can leverage the media. In fact, press releases are a good medium for highlighting your courses or material for the media to pick up.

Be sure you use integrate your PR exposure into your marketing strategy. Remember regardless of the tactic you must always think about how the tactic fits in your overall strategy. Think about what is going to happen next or what offer your PR tactics will link to.

Conclusion

What's Next?

You've been on quite the journey.

We covered How to choose a target market and create an ideal client. Then we went through how to become a "Weapon of Mass Attraction". From there we covered the "Rules of Engagement and Bonding", How to convert prospects into buyers, the importance of Delivering a "Broadway Show", and finally 3 Promotional Strategies.

By now you should have a the fundamental knowledge of how to create a marketing system that is designed to capture high quality leads and convert them into your ideal clients.

The only thing left to do now is take action on what you just picked up. With everything we included inside (and all the shortcuts) you should be able to start tomorrow and get your system up and running within the next 30 - 60 days.

I've armed you with everything you need to set the setup your marketing system, but I can't do the work for you.

The rest is up to you.

One more thing:

I want to hear your Success Story.

Write me at <u>omari@immediateactionmarketing.com</u> and tell me your success story after using the information from this guide (even if it's only 1 thing). I can't wait to hear from you.

Omari Broussard
Immediate Action Marketing

About the Author

Omari Broussard is a firearms instructor, strategic advisor, consultant, and mentor. He directly consults firearms instructors across the country and small business owners in Southern California. His consulting company, Immediate Action Marketing, focuses on helping firearms instructors create high converting marketing systems and authority positioning.

Omari is also a retired Navy Chief with over 20 years of service, a husband, father of 6, and life-long student.

Need a hand in achieving your business goals?

If you are here then you've found my strategies and tactics to be of some value to you and your business. And you are now either looking for some next steps or you want to leverage my knowledge and resources to accelerate your progress towards your personal and business goals.

I too was where you are right now...

Working hard everyday, hustling for new business, and in some cases "slaving" away.

My path to a dramatic turn when I invested in finding and retaining a mentor...

I can tell you with conviction the time and money I invested in getting a mentor catapulted my business forward in a major way.

However, I have to be upfront with you...I only have time to work with a select few. My current clients range from mid 6-figure to multi-million dollar earners. But, if we are a right fit I believe we can really take your business to the next level.

Go to the link below to submit your application. I will personally review your app and one of my team members will contact you to book a time for us to discuss your goals, challenges, and aspirations. If it makes sense, then the journey to achieving your business and personal goals will be just around the corner.

http://immediateactionmarketing.com/consultingapp

BONUS Chapter #1: Basics of Building a High Converting Website

The Basics of Building a Website

Imagine that you're going fishing. You spend all this time finding the right bait, learning where the fish are, and you've even told your family back home that they're going to have the most

delicious, fresh fish ever tonight. There's only one problem....the net you're going to use to capture the fish has a giant hole in it.

You can probably guess what happens next, right? You don't catch any fish. Your website is like that net. If you fail to set up your website properly then all those potential customers you drive to it will never convert and become PAYING customers. In today's world, your website should be the #1 source of leads, so you need to focus time, money, and energy there if you want to have a successful firearms instruction business.

In fact, the statistics show that 90% of your new customers have looked you up online before they call which is why I tell all firearms instructors that the biggest goals for your website are to:

1) Build Trust and

2) To establish a relationship with a potential customer before they pick up the phone and

If you can implement everything that I tell you in this chapter, then I promise you're sales cycles will be shorter, you'll get fewer people price shopping you, your classes will fill up faster, you'll close more business than you ever thought possible, and your firearms business will be one of the few who truly make money.

WordPress is King

This chapter is going to be more technical than most of the other chapters in this book so try to stay awake as I know that most of this stuff can get boring if you're not the technical type. I personally am not a very technical person, so I won't use a lot of jargon, and I'll do my best to keep it fun, but with that being said this is probably not the most exciting part of the book but it's one of the most necessary.

Now there are a lot of Do-It-Yourself website companies out there like Weebly, Wixx, GoDaddy, VistaPrint, etc., but if you're trying to build a serious online presence, then there is no better Content Management System than WordPress.

Today, WordPress is the gold standard when it comes to building your website and some of the biggest companies in the world use WordPress.

What is WordPress?

I'm going to make this explanation super simplified. WordPress is basically a FREE platform that you can use to build your website on. WordPress was initially created as a platform for people to create a blog and over the past few years, it has revolutionized the web design world and now it is the #1 platform on which to build websites.

One of the reasons it has become so popular, and I don't know if this is by luck or by design, is because it is incredibly search engine friendly. Google LOVES WordPress and with Google's new love of fresh, relevant content WordPress has grown tremendously.

The other reason that WordPress has become the #1 platform to build a website on is because WordPress is FREE and what's known as "Open Source". Open Source means that anyone has access to it and can make changes, updates, revisions, and IMPROVEMENTS to WordPress as they see fit. You have an entire planet of incredibly talented designers and developers who are all using WordPress and are making it better.

With that many people all working to make WordPress better it's no wonder that this platform has evolved so quickly.

The "1-Second Rule"

You may have heard that you have 3 seconds to capture someone's attention when they come to your website, and if you can't get that person to recognize that you have the content they're looking for in that 3 seconds, then that person will leave and never come back.

I'm here to make this even more mind-blowing for you. Throw out the 3-second rule. We now live in a world of the "1-Second Rule". With all the distractions in our lives and the fact that we all want immediate gratification, I believe that you have just 1 second to get someone's attention once they get to your website.

That means that if someone goes to Google, types in "Firearms Instruction San Diego", finds your website, and then clicks the link to your website, you only have ONE SECOND to show them that a) You have what they need, b) You are an expert, and c) You can help them RIGHT NOW.

You're probably wondering, "How in the world do I accomplish this in just one second?!"

Well, it's easier than you think and it starts with an easy navigation. You need to have a super, easy-to-read navigation that shows your services, your story and gets people to click through on the website, so they stay there. The navigation menu (this is what people often refer to as the "tabs" that link to the other pages on their website) should run at the top of your website and should run from left to right.

Your website needs to be an unbelievably sticky "net" to capture all your web traffic. If you've never done this before, then I highly recommend that you consult an expert web designer who understands MARKETING, who can help you implement a design and a user experience that creates stickiness and helps you beat the 1-Second Rule.

Here's another tip to help you improve the stickiness of your website. Have pictures that capture attention. Great images can captivate your audience and entice them to stick around. Think about the last website that you went to and after you got there, you decided to stick around. I'll give you a little hint: SEX SELLS. If you can somehow integrate images that have good-looking men and women, then your stickiness will improve.

For your Firearms Business, you MUST include photos of your facility and images of your students in the classes. You must show your potential clients that you have worked with previous clients just like them, that you've taken them from novice to expert, and that you can help them do the same thing.

Another thing is that you don't have to reinvent the wheel when creating your website. As a firearms business owner, you don't have to create some fancy, innovative website that the world has never seen before. Keep it simple.

When we do websites for clients, we ask them to find a website that they like and that they would want to emulate. We never blatantly copy someone else's site, but if there are elements that are generating business for someone else and we can "swipe" that style, then that's exactly what we do. I encourage you to do the same.

Find a firearms business who is doing really well and then model your new website after them. We've done sites that are inspired by some of the top firearms instruction companies in the world and who are crushing it, have spent thousands of dollars on their marketing, and then we

"Swipe" and leverage their experience for our firearms clients.

Lastly, incorporate a video on your website. The statistics show that a website video will get viewed, on average, for 2 MINUTES!! 2 minutes versus 1 sec. That is unbelievably powerful and so if you want to overcome the 1-Second Rule then by simply putting a quality video on your homepage you will increase your stickiness.

Make Your Contact Info Easy to Find

Another huge factor in creating a great website that generates revenue is ensuring that your contact information is easy to find on every single page. The best place to put this is in the upper right hand corner or the website.

People read right to left, top to bottom, so by putting your contact info in the upper right hand corner you are placing that important information in a great location that will definitely If you REALLY want to stand out, add a "Call to Action" next to the contact info. Have it say "Call Today" or "Free Consultation" or "Text Me for A Free Class" or whatever. People like to be told what to do when they come to your website so by simply putting a call to action in the upper right hand corner next to the contact information you can get a massive impact on It seems simple, but trust me...it works.

Put Up a Blog

You need to think of your website also as a "channel" for you to connect with people and enabling a blog on your WordPress website is the most important way for you to update content. From a marketing standpoint, the content on your "Pages" is not nearly as important as the content in your WordPress blog "Posts".

You should be updating your blog at least once a week, but if that's too much shoot for twice a month. Do it consistently and you'll be amazed at how quickly you can add more pages to your site and all of these pages give you another opportunity to be found online by potential customers.

The blog is also a way for you to position yourself as an expert in your industry. Here's a little hint: You don't even need to create your own content to be an expert. Look at Oprah. She doesn't really "create" content. She is like the world's most successful syndicator of other people's content. You too can become an expert in your field by syndicating awesome content that other people have created.

Just make sure that you "Source" and link to all the articles that you syndicate!I think this is probably the third time that

I've talked about video and it's for good reason. As of 2015, if you have a video on YouTube, it is 50 times more likely to be ranked on the 1st page of Google compared to an article. Furthermore, people spend on average, 20 minutes on YouTube when they go to YouTube AND YouTube is the #1 Search Engine on the planet. More people are searching on YouTube now than on Google!

If that doesn't get you excited about video then you need to smack your head against the wall. We are in the age of video and you need to jump on the bandwagon immediately. Once you post your video to YouTube, then you can easily post that video on your WordPress website. It is incredibly easy to do and your new video will keep people on your website longer and the longer they are on your site, the better chance you have to turn them into a customer. So put video on our website!!

Importance of Mobile

Did you know that there are more smartphones and tablets sold in the United States than laptop computers? Did you know that on average, 30% of all website traffic is coming from a mobile device and this number has been doubling every single year? And did you know that in some industries, the CURRENT mobile traffic to websites can be as high as 60%?!!

In April 2015, Google came up with their MobileGeddon Algorithm update which penalized people who did NOT have a mobile-friendly (also known as Responsive) website.

Mobile is an astronomically important aspect of your online presence that you need to be focused on. The first step is to ensure that your website has a "mobile-friendly" version which basically means that the screen size changes on a mobile device and tablet to make it easier for people to read. You can get a mobile plugin for your website from a company like Dudamobile (www.DudaMobile.com) or you can make sure that your website is utilizing what's called "Responsive Design". (When we build our websites we make sure that all of the sites we build are utilizing "Responsive Design")

Mobile traffic will only continue to increase so make sure that your website has a mobile-friendly version or you will be losing out on potential business.

Google Analytics

Smart marketers are obsessed with analyzing data also known as "analytics". Lucky for you, Google has a free tool called "Google Analytics" that you can install on your website so that you can monitor all the data about the people that come to your website.

This is extremely important, and I highly encourage you to install Google Analytics on your website as soon as you get your site built.

The Link for Google Analytics is www.google.com/analytics/ and again it is FREE. You'll just need a Gmail account (also free) to register.

With Google Analytics you can track things like:

- What location (cities, states, countries) that people are looking at your website from

- How many people are coming to your website and how many pages they are looking

- What pages people are reading

- How long they are staying on your website

- How many people are looking at one page and leaving vs. reading one page and then reading other pages

- How they are finding your website. Is it from google search? Another website that links to yours? An article you wrote? Etc.?

- How many people came to you from a mobile device.

- And much, much more!

Imagine this scenario. Let's say that you are a Firearms Instructor in San Diego, CA and you have Google Analytics installed on your website. The data shows that 60% of your web traffic is coming from Yelp and then 20% of your web traffic is coming from a blog article you wrote about "Firearms for Pregnant Women". Coincidentally, you've noticed that your sales have dramatically increased for people telling you they found you on Yelp and that you're noticing a huge increase in the number of clients who are asking about your

"Firearms Class for Pregnant Women" training services.

Hmmmm.....very interesting!

So what would you do? How would you respond to this data and make an educated, business decision?

Here's what I would do. I would look at advertising on Yelp so that I could get my business in front of thousands more people. AND, I would also look at doing Google AdWords for "Firearms Classes for Pregnant Women" keywords (ex: "Firearms training for women", "firearms training while pregnant", "how to protect your pregnant wife") and then I would also start doing a hell of a lot more blog articles on Firearms Instruction for Pregnant women.

Maybe even create a new VIDEO on Firearms Training Exercises that are proven to help if you're pregnant.

See what you could do here?!!

Google Analytics can show you how to make great business decisions so therefore it can be one of the best tools in your marketing arsenal. So install Google Analytics on your website and get on your way to becoming a SMARTER and MORE INFORMED firearms business owner!

Well, I've given you the crash course in creating a lead generating magnet for a website. If you do what I've just taught then I promise you will be head and shoulders ahead of your competition. If you want to learn more about this you can check out my bestselling book "It's Not JUST A Website" on Amazon.com or you can call us at WebsiteIn5Days.com at 1-800-935-3168. I really appreciate you investing in yourself and learning how to be a kick ass firearms training business owner.

BONUS Chapter #2: How to leverage Strategic Relationships

Why build strategic relationships

Every successful business understands and leverages strategic relationships to extend their reach in the marketplace. In this section, we are going to cover a few ways you can increase your authority, expand your market share, and increase the effectiveness of your marketing with less time and upfront investment.

Joint Ventures

Joint ventures are when two businesses collaborate to make more profit by sharing each others resources. An example of this method for firearms instructors can be found when an instructor connects with a local range. The instructor benefits because of the range, access to range resources (including list of customers), and more exposure to the market.

The Range benefits because the instructor can help the range gain more exposure to audience of the instructor, the instructor brings fresh material to the range's customers, and the endorsement from the instructor can increase membership and gear sales for the range. Ranges provide a the facility for training, instructors are the connection between the range and the clients.

The reality is that most ranges hire their own instructors to teach courses at the range. By hiring instructors, ranges can ensure training is compliant with their standards, thus lowering the risk for liability. However, the embedded instructors aren't able to build their own audiences which limits the ranges lead generation.

[NOTE: If you are a range owner or manager with instructors, it would be a good idea to let your instructors build their own audiences using the strategies in this book.]

As an independent instructor you bring a level of value to a range because you have the ability to give the range access to a new audience, which lowers the marketing cost for the range. You also have the ability build a deeper connection with the market. Remember, people like to do business with people not businesses.

Other joint venture relationships can be made with other instructors. For example, I did a concealed carry course with a friend who was certified in my state to conduct the mandatory ccw certification. We split the day up into 2 parts. He did the certification course and I conducted a 4-hour block on the fundamentals of defensive shooting. Since it was in his home turf, he was able to get more excited clients. It gave me more exposure in my state versus my city. It also gave me access to a number of people to market my specialty courses too in the future.

There are many ways to develop joint venture relationships. Here are some tips on creating profitable joint ventures:

Have your marketing materials ready to go. Don't leave it up to the host to market your course.

Always think WIN-WIN. Joint ventures are designed so that both parties receive benefit.

Go above and beyond. You not only represent your company, but also the other party as well.

Don't complicate the joint venture. Avoid making the relationship complicated, but ensure both parties have clarity on the project. Leave no question unanswered.

Strategic Alliances

I like to define "affiliate" relationships as "Strategic Alliances." A Strategic Alliance is where you align your company with another for mutual benefit. For example, let's say there is a piece of gear you've used for years with great results. Many gear companies have programs where they will pay you a commission for recommending their products.

This is a great way to get extra revenue in your business. It's also good to increase your companies value to your clients. I mentioned early the book that you want to become the "one-stop-resource" for your audience. And since you are more than likely to recommend gear to your students, it's a good idea to have strategic alliances with the company's you support. There is also an increased perceived value in your company when you align yourself with recognized brands in the industry.

Sponsorships

Sponsorships are where you receive support or resources from another company in return for exposure to your market. Companies know how expensive and difficult it is to get new customers. Some companies have a budget set aside for sponsorships of events, athletes, etc.

You don't just have to look within the firearms industry for sponsors, you can go to other local businesses in your area. One year I did an event and was able to get a number of sponsors to help cover cost. The range facility I used gave use a number of range lanes at no cost as a form of sponsorship. After the course I recommended the attendees shop at the range's pro-shop and of course they did. It was a win-win for all of us.

Sponsorship is also a way for you to acquire exposure and customers. You could sponsor a youth sports team in the community. Even amateur and pro athletes need sponsors, are there any in your town? What about community events in your area? By sponsoring events, you could have your banner right next to a well-known brand in your area.

Joint ventures, strategic alliances, and sponsorships are powerful ways to position your company and lower the cost of acquiring new clients. These strategies alone could double or triple your business within the next 12 months. Good Luck!

Made in the USA
Lexington, KY
15 February 2016